Christine Henriksen

illustrated by Emily Lynch Victory

Text copyright © 2020 by Christine Henriksen
Illustrations copyright © 2020 by Emily Lynch Victory

Published by Sakora Studio LLC
PO Box 23
Winsted, MN 55395
https://sakora.studio

Sakora Studio and the "Sakora" logo are trademarks belonging to Sakora Studio LLC.

The opinions expressed in this manuscript are solely the opinions of the author and do not represent the opinions or thoughts of the publisher. The author has represented and warranted full ownership and/or legal right to publish all the materials in this book.

All rights reserved. No part of this book may be reproduced, transmitted, or stored in whole or in part by any means graphic, electronic, or mechanical, including photocopying, taping, and recording, without prior written permission from the publisher.

First paperback edition 2020

ISBN: 978-1-950001-06-4 (pbk)
ISBN: 978-1-950001-07-1 (hc)

*To my caring family and friends.
This journey was made possible because of your care and prayers. Thanks also to God for guiding me through all of this, and a special thank you to my donor and donor family.
—Christine*

*To my mom and siblings for being the best caregivers.
—Emily*

One of my favorite things to do in summer is to find an open area on a sunny day, lie down, and stare at the clouds in the sky. I am very picky about the clouds. They must be those puffy white, cotton-looking clouds.

They move through the sky and change shape all the time. I usually see clouds shaped like animals, trucks, or things around the house. But one day, on my grammy and papa's farm, a most peculiar and wonderful shape appears.

It is one of those warm, sunny days at the farm. It isn't a big farm, but there are cows, chickens, pigs, a large garden, and a huge front yard with grass like green velvet.

I find my normal spot on the lawn. I wiggle around until I am comfortable on my bed of soft, green grass. I look up to the sky to begin my adventure of finding things in the clouds.

I am amazed at what I discover.

I can't help but stare.

I let my imagination soar, and soon I can hear this magnificent face talking to me. I decide to ask some questions to the large head.

I give my cloud shape a name. I decide to name it Metz, like my papa. Papa could answer any question. He was the smartest man I knew.

I ask my first question. "Metz, my brain is full of questions that no one has answered. My first question is why do big spiders always spin webs on the tops of juniper bushes, and when will those spiders leave?

"Grammy has junipers by the water spouts. When she asks me to turn the water on or off, I have to go through those junipers. I hate seeing all those webs. They give me the heebie-jeebies! How long will the spiders stay?"

I wait patiently for Metz to answer. Just when I think about giving up, I hear a deep voice answer me.

I lay there staring at the cloud as I hear these words:

"Spiders are very smart, but many people don't like them.

"Those spiders spinning fancy webs on the junipers are taking care of some very bad-guy bugs that people don't want near their homes.

I am satisfied with the Metz cloud's answer and can't wait to ask my next question.

"Grammy has a little garden on the side of the house. We always pick green beans, cucumbers, lettuce, peppers, tomatoes, and squash. My mouth waters just thinking about her fresh veggies. But there is a bunny that likes to eat from the garden. I don't want to hurt the bunny, but I want to save Grammy's garden. How long will that bunny eat our vegetables?"

Immediately,
I hear the answer.

"That bunny is not trying to annoy you. It only wants the same lovely foods that you like. The answer to your question is...

UNTIL

...you put a chicken wire fence around your garden, buried deep in the ground, and bend the top of the fence out.

"Without a fence, the bunny will not stay out of your garden. To be nice to the bunny, you can plant a few extra seeds away from your garden. The bunny will enjoy its own little garden."

My Metz cloud begins to float upward, but I can still see the strong mouth. I decide to ask one final question. There are so many ideas floating through my head. Which one is the most important to ask?

"Metz," I say, "my papa left us a few months ago. My grammy is getting weaker and paler. She seems tired, and her hair has gotten thin. I know she has been seeing a lot of doctors. How long will Grammy be with me?"

Although Metz is fading away, I clearly hear him say...

"UNTIL ...God decides it is time for Grammy to join Papa in heaven, Grammy will be with you and all the people who love her so much."

My Metz cloud is gone now. I see other shapes in its place. I think about the answers I heard. The best thing about Metz's answers is the one word he always uses: until. So when I think about the next time I might look for Metz, I decide I will wait...

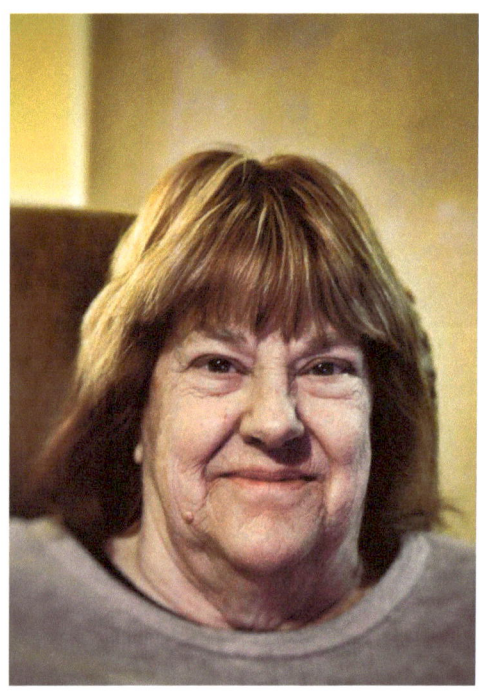

CHRISTINE HENRIKSEN is a former elementary school educator who always wanted to write children's books. Christine received her Master's in Literacy, taught for nearly forty years, and loved doing read-alouds with her students.

Family has always been at the center of Christine's life. This story was written from the heart, with Christine's parents as her inspiration. Christine lives in Casper, Wyoming, and adores her three children and four grandchildren.

In January 2017, Christine had a stroke shortly before what was supposed to be a routine surgery. Local doctors couldn't figure out what was wrong, so she went to Mayo Clinic in Minnesota. At Mayo, the doctors soon realized Christine's heart was failing. She was added to the heart transplant list and moved into the Gift of Life (GOL) transplant house just blocks from Mayo. She lived at GOL for nearly two years, and Christine said by far the hardest part was being away from her family.

"The days were long. I missed my family so much. It was because of all of that that I decided I wanted to write this book. Writing a book had been on my bucket list for a long time." So Christine started writing *Until*, thinking of all the students she'd had in her forty years as a teacher. "I spent so many hours thinking about the book *Until*. It held a lot of personal value because my mom and I used to watch clouds all the time. Metz is modeled after my dad, who is by far the strongest man I have ever known."

At GOL, Christine also met Emily's parents, and they all became friends. "[Emily's] dad made fun of me watching Jeopardy every day," Christine said jokingly. But when Emily's parents explained their daughter was an illustrator and found out Christine was writing a book, it seemed like fate. Christine said, "That is when I knew this was meant to be. And eventually, I met Emily."

Christine got a new heart in March 2019, the same day Emily finished her first sketches for *Until*. "Just can't believe how blessed I am," Christine said. "*Until* means so much to me. It grew from an illness into meeting genuinely wonderful people and an outstanding artist. I am so excited to share this book with children of all ages."

EMILY LYNCH VICTORY is a painter and illustrator enthusiastic about pattern. With degrees in both mathematics and fine art, she loves combining the two. Originally from Minnesota, Emily currently lives in Tampa, Florida, with her husband and three young, energetic, book-loving boys.

About two weeks before my first son was born, my dad got sick. Really sick. His local doctors tried to diagnose him but had no luck. The day I had my baby, my dad was taken to the hospital. I had no idea if my teeny Patrick would ever meet my big, strong dad, Patrick. It was such a happy, yet extremely hard, time.

My dad eventually went to Mayo Clinic in Minnesota to be diagnosed. A few days later he got the answer: Stage Four Lymphoma, a blood cancer that had spread to his whole body and bones. I'm happy to report that he's beat that cancer—twice.

My dad needed a stem cell transplant to clear out this recurring disease. It takes 100 days for someone's body to fully integrate a stem cell transplant. They need to be watched carefully by the doctors and kept in a clean environment with a caregiver. Because of all of that, my parents stayed at the Gift of Life House (GOL) near Mayo with my mom as my dad's caregiver. They made friends, rocked on the rockers out front, and made the best of being away from home.

At the GOL, my parents met Christine Henriksen, a former teacher who was waiting for a heart transplant. I met Christine, but I was extremely busy with my young sons and picture book illustrations. A year later, Christine was still waiting for a heart, my dad was getting stronger, and my boys were growing up.

During one of their nap times, I pulled up an email Christine had sent me with a children's story. I started to sketch out characters, clouds, and really dug in. I contacted Christine, and she was interested in making the project a book. The day I finished those first sketches, I called my mom. She told me Christine had just found out she had a heart donor!

The world works in pretty amazing, connected ways.

I hope you enjoy the book. It's my way of saying thank you to everyone who helped my family during that time and a way of hugging anyone who's been through a similar experience.

CPSIA information can be obtained
at www.ICGtesting.com
Printed in the USA
BVHW022330240820
587179BV00009B/166